TRUE STORIES OF
Teen Terrorist Recruits

Bridey Heing

Cavendish Square

New York

Published in 2018 by Cavendish Square Publishing, LLC
243 5th Avenue, Suite 136, New York, NY 10016

Cataloging-in-Publication Data

Names: Heing, Bridey.
Title: True stories of teen terrorist recruits / Bridey Heing.
Description: New York : Cavendish Square, 2018. | Series: True teen stories | Includes index.
Identifiers: ISBN 9781502631688 (library bound) | ISBN 9781502634047
(paperback) | ISBN 9781502631695 (ebook)
Subjects: LCSH: Terrorists--Recruiting--Juvenile literature. | Terrorism--Religious aspects-
-Islam--Juvenile literature. | Teenagers--Social conditions--Juvenile literature.
Classification: LCC HV6431.H43 2018 | DDC 363.325--dc23

Editorial Director: David McNamara
Editor: Caitlyn Miller
Copy Editor: Alex Tessman
Associate Art Director: Amy Greenan
Designer: Deanna Paternostro
Production Coordinator: Karol Szymczuk
Photo Research: J8 Media

The photographs in this book are used by permission and through the courtesy of: Cover ZUMA
Press/Alamy Stock Photo; p. 4 Patrick ROBERT/Corbis/Getty Images; p. 8 Balkis Press/Sipa via AP
Images; p. 10 RICKY GARE/EPA/Newscom; p. 12 Artur Widak/NurPhoto/Getty Images; p. 14
Ron Edmonds/AP Images; p. 16 Wikita/Wikimedia Commons/File:Little Insurgent Monument in
Warsaw 01.JPG/Public Domain; p. 26, 30 MATT BROWN/AFP/Getty Images; p. 28 Adam Pletts/
Getty Images; p. 34 Wolfgang Kumm/picture-alliance/dpa/AP Images; p. 37 Sam Farmar/Getty
Images; p. 39 GIANLUIGI GUERCIA/AFP/Getty Images; p. 41, 63 Pavalena/Shutterstock.com;
p. 43 CIAT/Wikimedia Commons/File:Pineapple farm lo (4108919878).jpg/CC BY SA 2.0; p. 44,
47, 83 AP Images; p. 49 AFP/Getty Images; p. 53, 56 Jonas Gratzer/LightRocket/Getty Images; p.
61 Jan Kvita/Shutterstock.com; p. 64 Alamy Stock Photo; p. 67 Al-Furqan Media/Anadolu Agency/
Getty Images; p. 68 Good/TNS/Newscom; p. 70 Europics/Newscom; p. 73 Metropolitan Police/
AP Images; p.79 TASS/Getty Images; p. 80 Pictures From History/Newscom; p. 90 Samir Bol /
Anadolu Agency/Getty Images; p. 93 ANDREW HOLBROOKE/Corbis/Getty Images.

Manufactured in China

CONTENTS

Teens on the Front Lines

The way wars are being fought is changing. Where once militaries met on the battlefield, today fighting is more complex, blurring the line between combatants and civilians. **Terrorist organizations** and **non-state actors** are able to create chaos and cause widespread suffering with a small group of leaders and improvised weapons. These organizations are also able to recruit and use a vulnerable population that can be manipulated into carrying out attacks without calling attention to themselves: teenagers.

Teens have played a role in conflict for as long as war has existed. Although today we think teenagers are distinct from adults and children, for most of history, young people were considered fully grown at a much earlier age. They therefore were able to participate in war. Today most countries have rejected the notion that youths under the age of eighteen can take part in conflict. But terrorist organizations around the

Opposite: As non-state actors and terrorist organizations have become driving forces in conflict, teenage recruits have been used in higher numbers. Here, a Congolese boy serves in a militia.

world do not. As a result, terrorists actively recruit young boys and girls to carry out a variety of tasks and missions.

Due to the hundreds of conflicts around the world that involve terrorist organizations or **militias**, another line that isn't clear is the difference between **child soldiers** and terrorist recruits. For many teens, the struggles and experiences between serving as a child soldier and carrying out acts of terror are extremely similar. In some countries, including the Philippines, the government will work with non-state actors, some of which might use teenage recruits to carry out attacks against opposition groups. This can make it even more difficult to draw the line between terrorist recruits and child soldiers. The difference is especially difficult to distinguish in cases when these young people are fighting on both sides of the conflict, as we see in Syria.

According to the organization War Child, there are an estimated three hundred thousand people under the age of eighteen taking part in conflicts around the world as of 2015. It is difficult to know how many of them are fighting on behalf of terrorist organizations rather than on behalf of government forces, or even how many of them are considered teenagers. The nature of terrorist recruitment is secretive and obscured, making it hard to know how many teenagers are fighting with a terrorist group at any given time or how many have died while carrying out suicide attacks.

Terrorist organizations are interested in recruiting teenagers for a variety of reasons, including their lack of criminal records and a still-developing sense of self, which makes them easier to manipulate emotionally. Young people are also less afraid than adults, meaning it's possible to encourage them to carry out deadly attacks. In some cases, such as in the

Lord's Resistance Army (LRA), fear is used to make young people cooperate with the organization. But in others, like with **ISIS,** a complex process of **radicalization** is undertaken to make the young person identify with the group and become loyal to its leadership. Sometimes terrorist organizations are able to provide pay or access to things like food, which can be very valuable in places where those kinds of resources are scarce. All of these methods are manipulative and coercive and can lead young people to make decisions they regret forever.

Like child soldiers, teenage terrorist recruits who are able to escape the cycle of violence that is part of belonging to a terror group must be treated with care and patience as they adjust to life after fighting. Some require medical care as they recover from injuries or mental health treatment as they work through trauma they experienced. Many of these young people miss out on crucial years of education. Some teenage girls become pregnant or have children due to sexual abuse at the hands of terrorists. Providing them with opportunity is one of the best ways to ensure they do not once again become radicalized or abducted.

While there is no question that young people carry out acts of violence on behalf of terrorist organizations, it is difficult to call them guilty. The nature of their circumstances makes them both victim and criminal, and many have to live with the emotional scars that dual identity causes. In this book, we will meet young people from across Africa, the Middle East, Asia, and elsewhere who have been forced to or have voluntarily joined terrorist organizations. We'll learn why they joined, what they lived through, and why they left. We will also learn about what resources they need to live normal lives after fighting, and how the international community has helped them in recent years.

CHAPTER ONE

Teen Terrorist Recruits Today

Teenage terrorist recruits fall under the same laws that govern the use of teenagers in combat. Recruiting minors as fighters is considered a violation of the Geneva Conventions, which dictate war crimes and crimes against humanity. But the definition of a child, and the way young people can be used by armed forces, is complicated. International statutes on the use of children in conflict are also difficult to enforce, relying on warrants that are difficult to act on within sovereign states. Often, a conflict must end before anyone can be prosecuted and held accountable.

The recruitment of people under the age of fifteen by either government forces or non-state groups was first made illegal in 1977, with the introduction of a legal document called

Opposite: Young people are often key targets of radicalization efforts. ISIS (*pictured*) is just one terrorist group that preys on teens.

A young Mai-Mai militia soldier carries a gun in the Democratic Republic of the Congo in 2004.

the Additional Protocols to 1949's Geneva Conventions. The 1989 Convention on the Rights of the Child also featured the prohibition of using people under the age of fifteen in war.

In 2002, the United Nations Children Fund (or UNICEF) stated that anyone under the age of eighteen taking part in conflict was a child soldier in the Optional Protocol to the Convention on the Rights of the Child

(OPAC), which is not legally binding. Most nations have signed on to the OPAC. But it has been controversial due to its allowance of states to recruit young people at the age of sixteen as long as they aren't sent directly into war. That same year, the Rome Statute of the International Criminal Court made it a war crime to use soldiers or fighters under the age of fifteen.

A HISTORY OF TEENAGE TERRORIST RECRUITS

Today, the international community is increasingly concerned about the risk of teenage recruitment by terrorist organizations due to the rise of social media and easy methods of communication. But although the means of recruitment have changed in recent years, the use of young people in conflicts has been practiced for centuries. The ancient Spartans were known to use young people through conscription beginning at the age of seven, and the Ottoman Empire created a special wing of their military for training children, called the Janissary Corps. Medieval European militaries also recruited children, either to serve knights or to fight themselves.

The history of teenage terrorist recruits is not so straightforward, due in part to the fact that the idea of terrorism as a unique phenomenon didn't emerge until the late 1700s. It wasn't until 1798 that the word "terrorism" came into use, marking a change in how we think about conflict. At that time, terrorism was defined by the Académie Française as a "system or rule of terror," and was a word applied largely to the government's use of violence to control its citizens. Although today that meaning has fallen out of fashion, the use

During the civil conflict in Northern Ireland, teenagers were recruited by both republican and loyalist militias.

of fear or terror to achieve political goals (such as controlling a population) is still one definition of terrorism.

THE NINETEENTH CENTURY

In the nineteenth century, the designation of terrorist was applied to groups of politically motivated armed groups that carried out attacks or assassinations. Many of these early groups, such as the Russian Narodnaya Volya and the Young Bosnia movement in Austria, used political assassinations to spark revolution or other large scale political changes. In the case of Young Bosnia that goal was met. The assassination of Archduke Ferdinand in 1914 is widely considered the event that began the First World War. That assassination is also an important example of the role of teens in terrorism. It was carried out by Gavril Princip, a nineteen year old.

THE TWENTIETH CENTURY

In the late nineteenth and early twentieth century, terrorism became a label assigned to groups by those in power. In turn this made it a tool for making dissent a crime. There have always been groups that use terrorism to target civilians and undermine authority. However, the rise of independence movements in reaction to colonial power in the early twentieth century complicated the way we understand terrorism. Groups like the Mau Mau in Kenya or the African National Congress in South Africa were fighting against oppressive regimes and were met with extreme violence—but after independence they went on to be regarded as heroes. Nelson Mandela, a celebrated human rights advocate and one of the key figures who fought against apartheid in South Africa, was considered a terrorist until public opinion turned against the South African government. These groups also gave rise to the heroic image

Traditional militaries have also long used teenage recruits, including Iran during the Iran-Iraq War, which ended in 1988.

of the **freedom fighter**, something that terrorist organizations use to recruit young people today.

One conflict where the lines between freedom fighter and terrorist were heavily blurred was during Ireland's struggle for independence from Great Britain and the subsequent conflict in Northern Ireland, which remained part of the United Kingdom. The Irish Republican Army (IRA) was a Catholic and republican organization that sought the unification of the Irish island under control of the southern Republic. On the other hand, Protestant groups like the Ulster Defense Association or Ulster Volunteer Force favored staying in the United Kingdom. Both sides carried out guerrilla attacks in cities like Belfast, including bombings and assassinations. In Northern Ireland, the IRA and loyalist paramilitaries frequently recruited young teenage boys to carry out attacks. There are reports of teenagers signing on as recently as 1999. Part of the desire to take part in the fight was its tribal quality, with groups positioning themselves as defending their community against an existential threat.

"There were loads of lads who lied about their age just to get into the movement. There were people who were jailed for IRA offences when they were fifteen. The Brits used to have a special wing in Crumlin Road jail for them—the Juvenile Remand Unit—which housed all those under seventeen. There were IRA volunteers killed in the conflict who were only fifteen and sixteen," Anthony McIntyre, a former teenage member of the group, told the *Guardian* in 1999. McIntyre was sixteen years old when he joined the organization by claiming to be seventeen to meet the official age cutoff.

THE RECRUITMENT OF TEENAGE GIRLS

Teenage girls have a long history of joining terrorist organizations. Groups like the IRA and the Tamil Tigers

This memorial in Warsaw is one of few that acknowledge the role of minors in conflicts around the world.

established all-women units that carried out bombings and other campaigns. But for many women who join terrorist organizations today, including those who join ISIS or are forced to join the LRA, equality doesn't wait for them. Instead, they usually experience sexual abuse and forced servitude to their male counterparts.

WHY TEENS JOIN TERRORIST ORGANIZATIONS

Anthony McIntyre joined the IRA by choice, and many teenagers around the world join other organizations by choice as well. But there are also many young people who feel coerced or forced to join terrorist organizations, something that we see with groups like ISIS or the Lord's Resistance Army. The lines between coercion and choice can also be unclear, as young people see themselves as having very few options in some situations. When a terrorist organization is able to offer money or food to families that otherwise don't have easy access, joining the group can seem like the safest way to ensure basic needs are met.

K. G. was sixteen when he was interviewed for a report by the United States Institute of Peace (USIP). He had just spent three years fighting with the Mai-Mai in the Democratic Republic of Congo. He expressed some confusion over whether or not he joined voluntarily. K. G. also highlighted the many reasons why young people are drawn to fighting forces, as well as the stark reality that he found when he had joined:

I think I joined freely. All my friends were already part of this group, even my uncle and many of my cousins. The Mai-Mai had long been around us; in fact they had built shelters next to our community in the forest. One day a friend of mine told me to come to the football grounds for a game. There we saw the Mai-Mai and they were telling us that today would be their pay-day, that a government official of the Congolese army would come and give them their monthly wages and if we joined, we could all get a share of that money. It didn't take me long to decide. In those days I was frightened, since our home was attacked almost every night by bandits and other rebel groups as well, what did I have to lose? Also my parents were too poor to send me to school anymore. My mind was made up fast, I joined my friends and from that day I never went home to my parent's house again. I know you think, how can I not think of home, but I never did. I was totally there in the forest with the rebels, I only thought of today and the drugs we got there. One time my parents tried to find me and buy me out with a goat, but I didn't even look at them. Home did not exist anymore you know, I was always under drugs from that day onwards. Also we had a purpose. You know North Kivu is very rich, many people come and want to rule us, they come and want our riches and we need to fight that, we need to fight for our freedom and to fight for our village. Our commander used to talk to us about this every morning when we met for morning assembly.

Young people can be susceptible to this kind of emotional manipulation, with some looking for a sense of self that groups like ISIS today or the IRA in the past were able to offer. By drawing young people into organizations using language rooted in a sense of community, identity, and higher purpose, groups are able to convince young people that they are undertaking heroic action that will make them celebrated and envied by their friends or families.

Often, teenage recruits are forced to take up arms on behalf of terrorist organizations. Human Rights Watch interviewed teenage boys who were abducted from schools in South Sudan, including Puok, who was sixteen years old when militia fighters broke into his school and kidnapped him along with hundreds of other teenage boys. Puok and his peers were given guns and a brief training on the day they were abducted, and then forced to take part in an attack:

At dawn the next day, they were taken to the nearby town of Mayom and ordered to attack government soldiers. Puok, who just twenty-four hours ago had been sitting in class, was terrified. He says it was an awful battle that lasted all day. "Shoot and move forward, shoot and move forward," the commanders ordered the boys. Eventually the town fell to their rag-tag force, but not before seven of Puok's classmates were killed and another ten injured.

Some groups, such as Sri Lanka's Tamil Tigers, will use the abuse of children to coerce their siblings to become fighters. Vanji was recruited by the Tamil Tigers in 1997, when he was just sixteen. Vanji left the group, but to get him to re-join, fighters abducted his younger brother. "They didn't release him, and they threatened to shoot if I reported his abduction. They also told me at the same time that I had to re-join," Vanji told Human Rights Watch in 2004.

But some young people join organizations or armies voluntarily, because these groups can provide resources or protection. R. H., a sixteen year old who joined a rebel militia in South Sudan, told Human Rights Watch, "We can die too, like everyone else; it's safer as a soldier. It is like a competition where do you run to, to be safe? You either die, or kill your enemy. Everyone is treated the same way, whether young or old."

Young people who decide to join armies or organizations often come to regret their choice. Tarik was just fifteen years old when he started fighting with rebels in Syria. But within a couple of years, he realized he had made a mistake and, as a soldier, had been feeding a cycle of violence that was destroying his country. Unlike many young people who change their minds, he was able to leave the group he had joined and return to his education. "My weapon now is my pen," he told SOS in 2016. "I wish to study architecture in university so that I am able to rebuild what we have all been destroying for years."

WHY TEENS ARE RECRUITED

There are also distinct reasons why young people are recruited by terrorist organizations and paramilitaries. For terrorist groups, young people without criminal backgrounds are less likely to be under scrutiny by authorities. This means they will more likely be able to carry out attacks without being detected. Teenagers who look particularly young are more likely to be seen as sympathetic and not draw attention to themselves in the way an adult might while carrying out an attack. Young people are also less aware of risks than adults. As a result, they are sometimes willing to undertake potentially fatal assignments without the hesitation an adult might feel. Young people on the front lines also pose a gruesome strategic purpose, as seen in the Iran-Iraq War when children were sent rushing towards enemy lines. Adults find it more difficult to kill minors in many cases. The Council on Foreign Relations notes:

> Trusting, vulnerable, and often intimidated, children can easily be manipulated, experts say. In combat, children can be daring and tenacious, particularly

when under the influence of drugs—a common practice—or when compelled by political or religious zeal. Child units can greatly add to confusion on battlefields, slowing opposing forces' progress. Children have also been used as scouts, messengers, minesweepers, bomb-makers, and suicide bombers. Child units are also effectively used as advance troops in ambush attacks.

UNDERSTANDING THE IMPACT

For young people who have been forced to fight on the frontlines, the journey to wellness is long and often complicated. Time spent as child soldiers and terrorist recruits can have immensely detrimental impact on young people's mental health. According to a report by USIP, the rate of **post-traumatic stress disorder (PTSD)** among escaped young people who had been abducted as children by the Lord's Resistance Army in Uganda and spent more than one month with them was as high as 48 percent. (Around 8 percent of their peers who had not been abducted had been diagnosed with PTSD.) Among those surveyed, the number of traumatic life events they experienced was shocking:

The most common traumatic life events of those who had been abducted were … forced to loot property and burn houses (48 percent), forced to abduct other children (30 percent), forced to kill someone (36 percent), forced to beat, injure, or mutilate someone (38 percent), caused serious injury or death to somebody else (44 percent), experienced severe human suffering, such as carrying heavy loads or being deprived of food (100 percent), gave birth to a child in captivity (33 percent of women), were threatened to be killed (93 percent), saw people with mutilations and dead bodies (78 percent), experienced sexual assault (45 percent), experienced assault with a weapon (77 percent), and experienced physical assault including being kicked, beaten, or burnt (90 percent).

The same report had similar results for experiences young girls lived through:

> 98 percent of girls had been threatened to be killed when disobeying, 98 percent had thought that they would be killed, 99 percent only narrowly escaped from death, 72 percent had been sexually abused by the rebels (in most cases forcefully "being given as a wife" from the age of thirteen years), 65 percent witnessed people being killed, 44 percent of the girls witnessed people being mutilated, 18 percent of the girls participated in killings, and 7 percent were forced to participate in killing own relatives. On average, the girls experienced twenty-four traumatic events during captivity.

Traumatic events like those seen by young terrorist recruits can have a lasting impact on their mental health. For young people, mental health issues like PTSD and others can cause life-long issues and make adjusting to life after fighting difficult.

Often, young recruits have been taken out of school and forced to endure horrific circumstances that can leave them physically or mentally unwell. They are also without skills and networks that other young people can rely on. Taken together, their needs are complex and comprehensive, requiring attention to their mental and physical health and on skills that will make them stable. Human Rights Watch spoke to young people who once fought against ISIS, but now face an uncertain future: "A boy in another camp said he joined the Yazidi militia when he was fourteen 'to kill some ISIL' and fought for nearly two years, but that now, [he says,] 'I have no job. I have no idea what I'll do.'"

NEWS COVERAGE OF TEEN TERRORIST RECRUITS

Child fighters have attracted a great deal of news coverage in recent decades, particularly with the emergence of the Lord's Resistance Army in Uganda in the 1980s and 1990s. With the rise of ISIS and their use of social media to recruit young people from around the world, news coverage of teenage terrorist recruits has been widespread and frequent. Their stories have also been profiled in both fiction and nonfiction books, movies, and television shows. But the coverage focuses most on shocking stories of brutality and fear. This does little to help the public understand the complex realities faced by young people who join terrorist organizations either by choice or by force.

Less attention is given to the long process of recovery than the immediate horrors the children experience, making it unclear how difficult the journey to wellness is. At the same time, stories about young people becoming terrorists can inspire fear in communities where recruitment is taking place. Teenage refugees or other vulnerable populations are demonized as a result. ISIS is working hard to recruit teens around the world. And fears about radicalization among refugee populations can shape the way resources are allocated to vulnerable communities. It can also affect how quickly young people are rehoused. The media coverage of terrorism and teen refugees contributes to a sense of threat from these populations. This makes it all the more important for well-rounded and nuanced coverage of the issues surrounding teenage terrorist recruitment.

This treatment of young people by the media has a significant impact on the lives of refugees and others seeking safety from ongoing fighting. Negative coverage can create fear in potential host countries, where teenagers are seen not as children but as possible sources of danger. This can shape government policy in a way that leaves these victims at a disadvantage or without access to resources. Meanwhile, in their home countries, young people can internalize messages that suggest hatred or anger at terrorist recruits. Young people who are coerced or forced to join terrorist organizations may come to feel they will not be given help or welcomed back into their societies if they are able to escape.

CHAPTER TWO

Teens in the Lord's Resistance Army

The Lord's Resistance Army has become the primary example of the use of children and teenagers by a terrorist organization. The group, led by Joseph Kony, has been recruiting teenagers and kids by force for decades and making them take part in extreme acts of violence that routinely shock the world. Despite progress to combat the group in Uganda, the LRA has remained a regional terrorist group that attacks civilians, abducts young people, and evades international efforts to hold them accountable.

Peter Singer, a Brookings Institute Fellow, has called the LRA "effectively a cult with a core of just two hundred adult members." Estimates put the number of young people abducted by the LRA at around twenty-five thousand, although it is unclear if this number is accurate. In order to make the teenagers take

Opposite: The Lord's Resistance Army has been active since the 1980s and has become known around the world for using children and teenagers as fighters.

part in fighting, the LRA uses violence to inspire fear and a cult of personality around Joseph Kony to inspire loyalty. At the same time, the LRA leads the young people they recruit to believe they will be rejected by their communities for the acts of violence they take part in, which keeps these teens and children from leaving the LRA.

THE LRA IN UGANDA

The Lord's Resistance Army has its roots in the Holy Spirit Movement, a rebel group founded by Alice Lawkena in 1986 to combat the oppressive government of Yoweri Museveni. Lawkena's militant group was built around directions Lawkena supposedly received from God. When Lawkena was forced into exile in 1988, rebel leader Joseph Kony usurped her authority and recruited her Holy Spirit Movement followers into his own group, the LRA.

Joseph Kony has evaded authorities for decades and developed a cult of personality around him that is used to manipulate teen recruits.

From its earliest days, the LRA was rooted in near worship of Kony, who claims to be able to read minds and speak directly to spirits. He and his followers sought to overthrow the Ugandan government and rule the country through Christian teachings and tribal custom. But Christianity as Kony interprets it is much like Islam as interpreted through ISIS: violent and cruel. The LRA have long targeted civilians rather than government forces, and in 1996, the Ugandan government had to evacuate much of North Uganda after the military was unable to adequately stop the LRA from attacking villages.

Despite peace talks with the government, international arrest warrants, and large-scale military operations to stop them, the LRA and Joseph Kony have been able to evade justice for more than thirty years. Between 1987 and 2007, it is believed that the LRA killed around ten thousand people and abducted over twenty thousand minors to join their ranks, whom they abused, tortured, and plied with drugs and alcohol.

The LRA, which has largely been pushed out of Uganda and into Sudan, the Central African Republic, and the Democratic Republic of Congo, is known for mutilating civilians and using sexual violence as a tool of war. Their cruelty is made even more shocking by their reliance on children and teenagers as fighters. F. O., who was thirteen when he spoke to the United States Institute for Peace researchers in 2006, was kidnapped at eleven years old and forced to take part in extreme violence immediately:

At age eleven, I was abducted and that same day they made me kill three of my uncles ... We were often starving, since there was no time to find food. Once we had to ambush a bus with civilians on the road towards Atiok to get hold of food; many people died and got burnt. Two days later we were asked to attack a camp. We were told to bring food and girls; we found three, but I was forced to kill two since they couldn't manage to carry the heavy loads and keep up. It wasn't long after that incident in the same year that I got a chance to escape during a battle with the UPDF.

Young people make up the vast majority of the LRA's forces; only a few hundred adults are believed to be part of the group.

According to Human Rights Watch, the LRA often abducts children in large groups, or brings together teens and children to create groups of recently abducted fighters. They are put through tests of marches and other physical activities, and those who fall behind are killed by their peers. This instills fear in the young people, and makes them too scared to try to run away. They are also beaten before being made part of the fighting force, as Mark T. (who was abducted around the age of sixteen) told Human Rights Watch:

> They gave us 150 strokes of the cane, and eight slaps with the machete on the back. It was the soldiers who did the beating. For the cane we were made to lie on our stomach and then the soldiers would beat us on the buttocks. There were twenty-three of us. For the machete, we were made to bend over at the waist, and then the soldiers would use the blunt end of it to beat us on the back.

FORCING TEENS TO PARTICIPATE

As we've seen, the LRA uses forced violence almost immediately to make young people feel obligated to stay with the group. The teens who carry out these acts of violence, which can include killing family members or beating other children, believe they are guilty enough to be rejected by society. This idea is reinforced by the LRA.

Norman was twelve when the LRA abducted him while he and his father were returning home from their rice field. The LRA soldiers asked if the man with Norman was his father, but Norman said no, fully aware that if he revealed that it was he would be forced to kill his own father. Instead, the soldiers beat him brutally before taking him away into the jungle, where he was forced to take part in torture, murder, and other acts of violence.

A DAY IN THE LIFE
OF A TEEN LRA FIGHTER

For teens abducted and forced to join the LRA, there is no average day. It depends on whether the teen is a girl or a boy, whether or not the group is on the move to avoid the many operations to bring them to justice, and whether or not there are attacks that are planned. All of this creates chaos that makes it even harder for young people to escape or get help. They never know where or what they will be doing. But no matter what, the day starts early for LRA members. Josephine M. told Human Rights Watch that while being held by the LRA in South Sudan she had to begin working at six in the morning and continue until late at night.

On any given day, children and teens may be made to fight for the LRA and abduct other young people or carry out raids on villages for supplies like food or livestock. Training is also conducted for young people who are new to the group and can last for weeks. Sometimes young people are also put in charge of watching one another and carrying out punishments if the rules are broken.

Most young people are assigned duties, because the core adult forces of the LRA are very small in number. As a result, children and teens have to take on actual duties to make it possible for the group to survive, although most often they are charged with doing things to care for the adult commanders rather than their fellow teens or kids. This can include carrying goods or supplies, like water or ammunition, or going out on raids to take more supplies. Young people are made to carry arms and personal items for the commanders they serve, and they often have to carry the items over long distances when the group is avoiding military or other forces. When the group is able to stop for periods of time, young people have to dig fields or make charcoal by cutting down and burning trees.

Teenage girls are forced to help with household duties, like getting water or cooking. Many commanders have more than one wife, and wives often beat or abuse the younger girls who are assigned to help them. Some girls have to get up hours before anyone else to find sources of water—sometimes as early as four in the morning.

Multiple young people who escaped from the LRA have reported very little food or water is given to young fighters, despite their role in helping secure the goods. Hunger is widespread, and many young people die of starvation. With no beds, homes, or security, the night comes with its own terror, whether it be sexual assault for the girls or continued punishment for the boys. It is a cycle of pain and suffering.

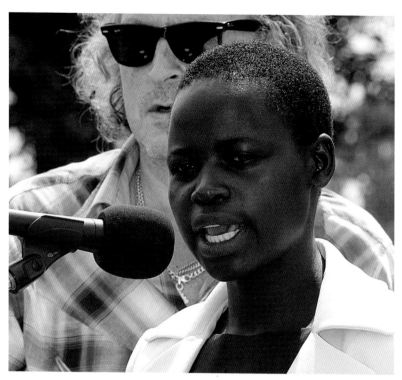

Young people who escape the LRA, like this girl named Hope, sometimes become advocates for those who are with the group. Some are used to encourage others to escape to safety.

"When you kill for the first time, automatically, you change," Norman told the *Telegraph* in 2014. "Out of being innocent, you've now become guilty. You feel like you're becoming part of them, part of the rebels."

Although much focus is on boys abducted and forced to take up arms as fighters, girls are also abducted and forced to take part in violence. A. A. was thirteen when the LRA abducted her, and was fifteen when the told USIP about her experiences in 2006:

> The commander looked around and saw me and my friend sitting in some distance and he said: "Call those two seated over there." He called us to come in front.

And he told us: "A girl should be killed by a girl. Get the sticks and beat her to death." I got so frightened and started to shake. I said: "I don't want to kill, I don't know how to do this, I have never harmed a person."

LEARNING NOT TO CRY

After being threatened for refusing to carry out the violence, A. A. did as she was told. The experience was deeply traumatizing, and she recalled in detail what took place, including the fact that she was threatened again when she became upset. Afterward, she joined some women who were with the group who both comforted her and taught her a lesson: don't cry:

Finally we were allowed to leave the place. I went to where people were seated. I sat next to an older woman. Girls who have freshly killed are not allowed to sit next to the boys. But there are older women, who have killed often and know what to do, so you sit next to them. She consoled me and she took me by the arm and told me not to cry. She said to me: "Stop crying or else they will kill you." She sat near me and held my hand. After you kill you shouldn't cry.

Asking teens to commit these acts of senseless violence serves multiple purposes. They can be used as a way to instill fear in the young people, and they communicate that if the teens try to escape or otherwise break the rules they, too, will be killed. By forcing young people to kill their own family or friends, the LRA makes it less likely they will try to return to their communities, either because their families are gone or out of fear that the former neighbors will reject them due to their violence. Killing is also a way the LRA promotes a **common identity**. After taking part in this kind of violence, young people are often welcomed into the fold of the group and made to feel as if they now belong.

Grace was fifteen when she was abducted from her school and forced to march with other teenage girls through wilderness. Along the way she was beaten and forced to take part in beating others. "I don't even know how to speak about it," she told radio station WBUR in 2012. "It was horrible. What they did to us is what should never be done to any human being."

For young girls like Grace, being abducted and forced to join terrorist organizations carries the threat of sexual assault and abuse, something Grace experienced during her time with the LRA. Some of the girls become pregnant, which can carry stigma if they are able to escape and return to their communities. It can also make them targets of continued violence by the LRA. Others are beaten and abused by the wives of commanders and fighters and forced to live in servitude to those who abducted them. Brenda O. was a teenager when she was abducted and given to Commander Ochang. When she escaped, she told Human Rights Watch:

> He didn't treat me very well. He would order young soldiers to beat me and two of the [others]. The commander would call to us to come and lie down. He would say, "Do you know why I am beating you?" We didn't know, so the soldiers caned us, fifty strokes. This happened every day. They beat us on the buttocks,

Teenage recruits are forced to take part in extreme violence and then told that their crimes mean they will be rejected by society.

but if you cry, they will beat every part of your body and not count the strokes.

MORE FEAR TACTICS

O. B., who spoke to USIP researchers in 2006, was fourteen when he was abducted by the LRA. His story is another example of the ways the group used fear to control the children they abducted. Along with a group of boys abducted around the time he was, O. B. was forced to lie on the ground while soldiers beat him. The reason for the abuse was that supposedly the young boys looked like they might escape. This lie was told to make the children think their captors could read their minds or otherwise guess at their intentions. This is a technique used by the LRA. By making the boys think their every move is being watched and could bring punishment, the boys censor themselves more closely and fear even thinking about fleeing. According to O. B., after being beaten hundreds of times, he was the only one of the group to survive.

WHEN TEENS ESCAPE

A fear of the consequences of escape is key to the LRA's program of brainwashing, but that doesn't stop some young people from trying to get away. Thousands have made it to centers and camps for displaced persons, and these young people have been able to help save others by sharing their stories. But their lives are difficult after escape, particularly if they do not have access to resources or programs that are designed to help them recover.

Children and teens who are found after escaping from the LRA are taken to government-run Child Protection Units, where they receive medical care depending on their needs. Some are then taken to rehabilitation facilities in cities to receive help from nongovernmental organizations or community members.

Other young people return to find their parents dead or gone and have few ways to care for themselves. In some cases, they are also ostracized by their communities. V. O. spoke to USIP researchers in 2008 after being abducted twice by the LRA. He was four years old the first time, and he was held for seven years. The second time he was thirteen years old and held for two years. At age eighteen, he was struggling to help care for his little sister while dealing with the psychological toll his time with the LRA had taken on him:

My younger sister Aciro doesn't get those problems that I have, when I forget everything and act in strange ways when the memories from the bush come back. We are alone, since my parents have been killed and living in a small hut in the camp makes life difficult when this thing comes over me. When my mind goes

Teenagers who escape the LRA often struggle with PTSD, anxiety, depression, or other mental health issues due to what they have seen or done.

away, then my sister runs out and locks me up in the hut. Later, when I have stopped acting out and lie down to sleep and stay quiet, she comes back. It can happen twice a day that I forget time and wake up in a strange place where I don't know how I got there ... Problem now is that people in the community think I am crazy and they want to take away our ancestral land from us, but digging and harvesting is the only source of income we have.

HELPING FORMER LRA FIGHTERS

Efforts have been made in Uganda to help teens like V. O. readjust to society and work through what they have experienced or have taken part in. Groups like Invisible Children and Save the Children work with local communities to educate people on how to help reintegration efforts and to help young people who have been victims of the LRA's system of abduction come to terms with what happened to them. But there are many threats for young people who have escaped the LRA, including the LRA itself, which often re-abducts fighters or punishes those who help them. Similarly, many children are abducted along with siblings, and live in fear of what will happen to their loved ones still with the LRA.

Some young people are able to return to something like their own lives. Norman, who narrowly avoided killing his own father, escaped shortly after taking part in the Kitgum Massacre, a mass slaughtering in a village in Uganda. Yet when he returned home, his parents found him thoroughly changed. He was violent, aggressive, and he told the *Telegraph* that he thought often about killing his own parents.

Norman and others were able to work through his transitional period due to programs like group play with other former recruits, where they are free to talk about what they are feeling without judgement. "When you play football with your friends, the former child soldiers, you say, 'I think destructive things. What about you? How do you feel?' They say, 'Even me, I feel the same.' And, for sure, you feel very good," Norman said. The groups are built on the idea that you "leave what you've done" behind you and look to the future.

Although Norman has been able to carve out a normal life, complete with a wife and children, he is still haunted by his time as a fighter. "I'm normal now. I'm just another member of the community. But the nightmare is there. I dream about someone coming to abduct me."

Many other young people have little hope for the future. Robbed of their education and health, they see little opportunity

The LRA began in northern Uganda. It has recruited members from neighboring countries, impacting thousands.

on the horizon. For young girls, sometimes they are forced into motherhood too young, such as Christine A. She told Human Rights Watch, "I'm not happy at all because they ruined me. I had to cut short my studies. I have no hope that I will one day be somebody. I gave birth to two children and was not prepared. I have two children and no means of survival. I worry about what will happen next."

John W. was sixteen when he talked to Human Rights Watch and shared a similar sentiment: "What disappoints me most is the future. Some seem to have things to do here, and a place to go, but for me, the future is blank ... What am I going to do?" It's clear that former members of the LRA sorely need help to achieve stability and regain their hope for the next chapter of their lives.

THE ECONOMIC IMPACT OF THE LRA

The economy plays a large role in how communities are able to help young people returning from terrorist organizations. In the parts of northern Uganda, South Sudan, Central African Republic, and Democratic Republic of Congo where the LRA is and was active, the economy tends to be weak and instable. At the height of the LRA's activity in Uganda, thousands were forced to flee their homes and live in camps, giving up land and jobs that had sustained them. Although many have returned and there are signs of progress in recovery (including multi-million dollar development and recovery plans launched by the government), rural and agricultural areas remain impoverished.

Even today, a decade since the LRA has been heavily active in northern Uganda, their terror has left behind a culture of fear and a lack of access to resources that makes economic growth difficult. What's more, young people returning from time with the LRA have often missed out on education and vocational training opportunities that makes securing high-paying jobs difficult, leaving them vulnerable to exploitation or even re-abduction if they live in insecure settings or camps. "Victims and survivors still grapple with serious mental health and psychosocial challenges and are

Rural areas in Uganda have been severely affected by the LRA. Pictured is a pineapple farm in western Uganda.

unable to engage in productive ventures. For many, the war still continues in their minds despite the guns falling silent," Jackson Odong of the National Memory and Peace Documentation Center said in 2016.

Poverty can create a cycle of struggle that leaves young people vulnerable to recruitment or abduction. In poor areas, security is often lax or non-existent, offering the LRA chances to return and abduct more young people. For those who do escape, their mental and physical health can go unaddressed, making it hard for them to feel truly safe or stable. Having missed out on educational opportunities or training, many are forced into low-paying jobs or prolonged unemployment, which can leave them vulnerable to further victimization.

CHAPTER THREE

Teen Terrorist Recruits in the Philippines

For decades, a civil conflict has torn the southern Philippines apart, resulting in widespread displacement and heavy fighting. The fighting is between the government, Islamist separatists seeking their own state, and communist insurgents who seek to overthrow the government. All of the major groups fighting in the Philippines have recruited children and teenagers to fight with them at some point, as we will learn below. What's more, all have made various vows to stop using teenagers in combat, some with more success than others.

COMBATANTS WHO RECRUIT TEENAGERS

While there are other groups fighting in the Philippines, the organizations that have been recruiting teenagers as of 2016,

Opposite: Despite efforts to demobilize teenage fighters, non-state groups in the Philippines continue to recruit fighters under the age of eighteen.

according to the United Nations, are the New People's Army, the Moro Islamic Liberation Front, and Abu Sayyaf. Abu Sayyaf and the New People's Army are considered terrorist groups by the United States and the Moro Islamic Liberation Front is classified as an "armed insurgent group."

THE NEW PEOPLE'S ARMY

The New People's Army is the military wing of the Communist Party of the Philippines, one of the world's oldest communist insurgencies. It was established in 1969 with the goal of overthrowing the government through irregular warfare, and it has since carried out attacks across the country. According to the BBC, around forty thousand have been reportedly killed by the NPA. The NPA was designated a terrorist organization by the United States in 2002.

The NPA uses several tactics to provoke the government, including killings, kidnappings, and extortion. The group's leadership lives in exile but claim that they lead the group from afar. Although the NPA is not particularly powerful today, with an estimated ten thousand members, they continue to recruit and use young people to carry out attacks and target civilians despite making pledges to stop doing so.

THE MORO ISLAMIC LIBERATION FRONT

The Moro Islamic Liberation Front, or MILF, is a splinter group formed by fighters who split with the Moro National Liberation Front (MNLF) in 1978. They are the largest Muslim rebel group in the Philippines, and despite seeking an independent Islamic state in the south, they have been engaged in peace talks with the government since 1997. Although there were hopes that a peace agreement that created a Muslim autonomous region in Mindanao called Bangsamoro would be signed in 2017, at time of writing that deal had not been finalized or signed.

Unlike the NPA and Abu Sayyaf, the MILF has been found by the United Nations to be committing to their pledge to stop using teenagers and children. As of November 2016, the group had met most benchmarks on their most recent action plan and leadership had agreed to start the process of demobilizing all minors under their command.

ABU SAYYAF

Abu Sayyaf is a relatively small Islamist group with radical ideology and potential links to groups like al-Qaeda. The group was founded in 1991 when fighters split from Moro National Liberation Front. Their goal is to establish an Islamic state in

Abu Sayyaf, an Islamist extremist group, is one of the most prominent recruiters of teenagers, who both volunteer and are coerced into joining the group.

Mindanao and the Sulu islands, but the government refuses to hold talks with them due to their criminal activity and terrorist actions. Abu Sayyaf has also been condemned by the MNLF and MILF.

The group largely relies on ransoms from kidnappings for money, and they often target journalists and foreign aid workers. They carry out bombings that target civilians, including a high-profile attack on a passenger ferry in 2004 that resulted in 100 casualties. Support for the group is limited across the country, but individuals in impoverished areas have been willing to work with the group in exchange for money. Abu Sayyaf not only recruits teenagers, but tortures or mutilates those that are accused of spying or otherwise being disloyal.

Reasons for Going to War

Unlike in the case of the LRA, many young people join terrorist organizations in the Philippines by choice. Some of them join to escape unsafe conditions, such as abuse from a family member or ongoing conflict near them. Others join out of a desire to have basic needs met. This is a phenomenon that is seen around the world. Terrorist organizations and paramilitary forces can sometimes provide stability or resource for young people who otherwise do not have it. Still others join out of a desire to get revenge on forces, including the military, responsible for killing their loved ones.

One young teen, who joined the NPA when he was just fourteen, told UNICEF that he did so in hopes of helping others and combating what he saw as a corrupt military that preyed on rural populations: "I joined to serve the people in the mountains. We protected them from violence and harm, from the government soldiers. These soldiers, they were abusive; that's why we kept watch. That was how we helped the people in the mountains."

In some cases, parents see joining these groups as a way forward for children who are misbehaving. One boy who joined when he was thirteen was encouraged by his parents to join the NPA after he dropped out of school and started spending time with other children they didn't approve of. He told UNICEF:

Some young people join groups like the NPA out of a desire to learn or help others and to escape abusive or bad home lives.

THE HISTORY OF THE CONFLICT IN THE PHILIPPINES

The civil conflict in the Philippines has been taking place for around fifty years. It encompasses two different conflicts, both of which involve insurgencies against the central government. The first involves the Communist Party of the Philippines (CPP) and the National People's Army, while the second involves the Moro Islamist separatist movement.

Fighting began in 1969, when the NPA broke away from the CPP after having served as its military wing. The group wanted to be more effective in their struggle to establish a Marxist democracy, and they began focusing their efforts in the rural areas of the country where poverty was rampant. In the decades since, the group has been involved in attacks on military outposts and assassinations. Despite peace negotiations with the government and ceasefires, there has been no full end to the fighting since 1969.

The Moro insurgency also began in 1969, when tensions between the government and Muslim rebels groups became violent. That year the Moro National Liberation Front was founded and began staging attacks on the government, and since then, other groups like the MILF and Abu Sayyaf have also been established to fight for an independent Muslim state in the south. More recently, groups like Abu Sayyaf and the newer, more radical Bangsamoro Islamic Freedom Fighters have been accused of aligning with terrorist groups like al-Qaeda, and they have rejected peace talks that would result in a largely autonomous Muslim region.

In mid-2017, fighting broke out between Islamist groups and government forces in the city of Marawi. The fighting came after the election of Rodrigo Duterte, a divisive leader who has been accused of extrajudicial killings in his war on drug dealing. Fighters in the Marawi area are believed to be linked to ISIS, and many teenagers were said to be among those who engaged troops in early battles. Although still developing at time of writing, the fighting signals that the conflict in the Philippines is far from over, despite efforts to secure peace.

When I stopped studying, I started hanging out with some boys. My parents told me, "Do not hang around with them because you might involved with what they were doing. You might end up doing something bad." … Then one day I heard someone say, "Who wants to join us in the mountains? Come with us, this will be for your own good so that you won't do something bad." I thought about it and told myself, "Since I wasn't doing anything because I didn't have a job and I wasn't studying, I will just join them so that I could avoid doing bad things." … There were also other children [who joined]. The children joined because their parents wanted them to. These were children who weren't doing anything. Their parents said, "Go to the mountains instead because that is better."

Some young people receive money for their families, particularly from the NPA. The possibility of payment is a draw for teens around the world, particularly in areas where there is little economic opportunity. The MILF does not pay their fighters or their families, with one teenage boy telling UNICEF, "I joined the MILF not for pay but for Allah." One sixteen-year-old girl, named Sonia, told UNICEF that she didn't necessarily have one reason for joining the NPA, but rather many reasons:

She claimed that there were several factors. These were threat of sexual abuse by an uncle, being forced to marry an old man, and the physical, verbal, and emotional abuse from her older brothers and sisters. All of these

Some teenagers return to their families after working with militias, but others remain in these groups for a long time. Pictured are NPA members.

are circumstantial factors. What triggered her to finally decide to run away and join the NPA was when her mother refused to believe her when she told her that her uncle attempted to rape her.

Although Sonia chose to join the NPA, she was startled to find how it changed her. Her own reactions to seeing death shocked her, and as she recovers from the trauma she experienced she continues to work through how being a soldier changed the way she sees the world. When another soldier was shot while fighting beside her, her first reaction wasn't fear or concern. Instead, she laughed:

> I laughed when I saw him and said, "Oh, he's dead!" ... I didn't feel ill when I saw a dead body; maybe I got a bit scared when I imagined that the corpse might suddenly open its eyes. I recently helped our housemother bury a child from the center that died at the hospital. I don't think that my reaction is normal.

Another girl told UNICEF that life came down to the simple idea of kill or be killed:

> I never knew for sure if I shot anybody. We were usually ambushed at night and I couldn't see if I hit somebody. Did you know that in the dark, bullets flash like fire? There were some who pretended to be tough after they learned that they killed someone. Their eyes would flash and they seemed to be very alert. But then I

noticed that they did not seem to be aware of what was happening around them. I think they were in shock. I saw a seventeen-year-old girl cry and pray to God to forgive her for what she did. There were those who found it easier to kill after the first one. They got used to it. It's kill or be killed.

EMPOWERED TEEN GIRLS?

While there is a significant focus on teenage boys abducted by the LRA in Uganda, there is a focus on girls recruited by groups like the NPA in the Philippines. This is in part because the NPA promotes gender equality in a way that few other such organizations do, and girls who leave the group report that they felt safer with the group than they did in abusive households. This feeling of safety is in stark contrast to groups in Uganda, Syria, and Colombia, among others, where young girls are often sexually and physically abused by terrorist and paramilitary groups. One girl told the Quaker United Nations Office that it was a rule made clear to them that men were expected to respect women:

In the seminar, it was made clear that it was absolutely prohibited to take advantage of women, for men to abuse women was not allowed. It wasn't even allowed to touch each other, to speak to someone of the opposite sex alone, especially in dark places, this was also prohibited. I felt very safe; I had no fear.

A sense of empowerment was an important part of why many girls joined the NPA. Many of them reported feeling as if they had no voice in their own lives and were marginalized within their families. Other groups, like the MILF, did not have this kind of equality, and instead relied on girls to do things like cooking and cleaning. With the NPA and some other groups, girls are given leadership roles that they may otherwise struggle to attain due to their gender and the limited opportunities they might have a result of poverty. One girl who joined when she was thirteen said, "They made me 'team leader' for a short time because they thought I was alert and

In some groups, including the NPA, girls are given more freedom and responsibility than they might have at home, including leadership roles.

smart. Then I was trained to become a medic. They taught me traditional ways of healing."

Aida's story shares similarities with the other girls who spoke of the opportunities the NPA provided. Aida was high school age when she joined the NPA and started relaying messages between commanders and fighters in the field. As a young girl in the southern Philippines, Aida felt she had few opportunities outside of joining the NPA. While in the group, she learned to read and write, and took on community organizing roles in rural areas. She told the Quaker United Nations Office that she was empowered in a sense, given confidence and security that she wouldn't have found at home. But after being captured by the military, she admitted that while she was still attached to the NPA, she was most interested in going home and get away from the high-pressure situations she was encountering on a day-to-day basis: "I really want to rest and be with my mother … The best is to go home. I have this feeling that I'd be able to forget about the movement … I just want to laugh. I was always crying [when I was in the movement]," Aida said.

Given the reasons why some young people decide to join these organizations, it can be difficult for them to find safety and security at home. Without access to basic resources like food or education, and for many living in fear of the military, life with an organization like the NPA could provide for their needs. Many of the young girls who join the group cited concerns about their safety or a history of abuse as a reason why they were quick to sign up—and that the protection of the group provided relief.

CAN TEENS TRULY "VOLUNTEER"?

No matter how teens who joined might make it seem, there is manipulation behind voluntary recruitment into terrorist organizations. The MILF plays on young Muslims' sense of duty to their faith to attract recruits, with one sixteen-year-old recruit telling UNICEF that he and others joined because it is an obligation. Another who joined at age twelve told how he was recruited:

> I joined the army four years ago when I was twelve years old. I was recruited by the Ustadz [the one who leads prayers at the mosque] in my community. I was told that the military/government was the enemy of the Muslims. I got to know Ustadz Yusuf when he attended the prayers in the mosque. I knew the Ustadz for almost a month or more. I was recruited in my municipality. The Ustadz asked me to join the jihad. I became a soldier voluntarily.

TERRIBLE RISKS FOR TEENS

Among the many risks of joining a terrorist organization in the Philippines, capture by the military is a big one. For teen recruits who are arrested or captured by the military, the line between perpetrator and victim is often erased, feeding fears instilled by the groups that the military will punish the young people harshly if they are captured. According to De Castro, there are accounts of young boys being beaten or tortured by military forces. One she spoke to, named Akbar, was seventeen when he fell into the hands of the military, who accused him of being part of the MILF:

> He was brought to the headquarters of the 4th Special Forces Company with four other men. During detention, he was boxed repeatedly by soldiers, his right foot was repeatedly burned with lighted cigarettes, his neck and legs were hit with the butt of an armalite rifle and his hands were tied for three days straight.

And according to a report by the United Nations, young people—even those who have never joined a terrorist group—are particularly at risk from ongoing conflict, both at the hands of the communists and Islamist extremist groups. In addition to teenagers being detained by the military on suspicion of being involved with terrorist organizations, there were incidents in which young people were directly targeted for sexual violence or other acts of cruelty:

> The United Nations verified the killing of six children and the injury of twenty-five. A third of the casualties were attributed to the Abu Sayyaf Group. For example, in May, a boy was beheaded by the Group in Basilan for allegedly spying. Two verified incidents were attributed to the Armed Forces of the Philippines, involving the killing of two children and injury of two others. On August 18, in Bukidnon Province, northern Mindanao, the Armed Forces of the Philippines killed five family members in front of their house, including two boys aged fourteen and seventeen years. Two injuries were

A DAY IN THE LIFE OF A TEEN TERRORIST RECRUIT IN THE PHILIPPINES

Life a teenage recruit for groups like the NPA revolves around spreading the group's message in rural areas. Teen recruits' lives are full of hard work and demanding hours, often starting in the early hours of the morning and not ending until late at night. They do not go to school, and instead spend their days taking on difficult physical labor and public speaking roles as they work to rally support for their organization.

Young people wake up before dawn to train and exercise, sometimes as early as 4:00 a.m. Then after breakfast they receive their assignments for the day, which could include organizing rural communities, helping people take care of problems around their homes or farms, or working with the rural youth to try to recruit them. In exchange, the rural populations often take care of the fighters, providing them with medicine, food, and other goods they might need. This relationship is crucial to the survival of groups like the NPA, and the role of the young recruits in maintaining it is no less important.

Young recruits also take part in criticism groups, which are held throughout the day to provide feedback among peers about their work, philosophy, and other issues. At the end of the day, the camp usually has to be moved, and young people are responsible for carrying large loads of goods for miles to the next campsite. Although there wasn't much down time, one girl told the Quaker United Nations Office that when they did have time to relax, they forged deeper bonds:

When there were times when we didn't have work to do, we would relax, there would be lots of jokes and we would sing together. To everyone, if you are upset about something or someone, this can be discussed.

Teens in rural areas of the Philippines are targets of terrorist recruiters.

Even relationships with women can be discussed. If you want to enter a relationship, then the man can approach the woman.

The routine changes if the group is getting ready to fight. All teenage recruits, boy or girl, are given assignments, including radio communication, intelligence gathering, handling and using technical equipment, spying, or other roles. While their day-to-day lives are challenging but unthreatening, battle forces these teenagers to risk their lives for the group, and many of them die or witness the deaths of peers.

For most young people, their experiences with the NPA and other groups were a mixed bag. On one hand, they received skills and knowledge they would not have otherwise been given access to, like literacy, technical skills, or organizing. Yet in exchange, they were forced to take part in warfare, a trade that is not only unfortunate but unfair. This exchange speaks to the complex cost and benefit that these young people weigh when they choose to join the NPA.

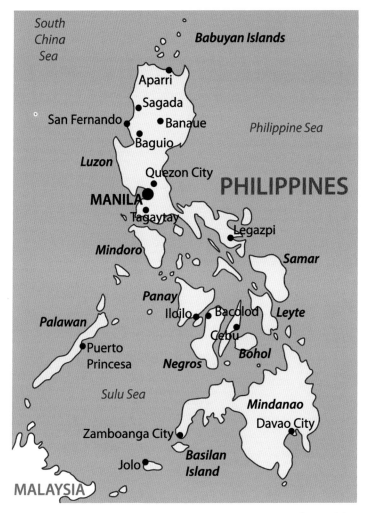

The Philippines has more than seven thousand islands. Some risk being taken over by terrorist groups.

attributed to the Magahat paramilitary group, one killing to NPA, and one injury to the National Police.

As lack of security plays a large role in recruitment, these stories illustrate further the complex way young people have to find comfort and safety where they can find it—and why it is important to ensure their safety in noncombat situations to end recruitment of teens in the Philippines.

CHAPTER FOUR

Teens in ISIS

Since emerging in the Middle East in 2013, ISIS has become one of the most formidable terrorist organizations currently active. It has a network of aligned groups around the world and the capacity to recruit strategically from countries like the United States and from countries across Europe. ISIS has proven their ability to recruit teenagers by force and voluntarily. The group has demonstrated a willingness to manipulate young people into carrying out deadly attacks and a blatant cruelty in punishing those who decide to leave the group. Their use of social media has made them a concern to countries around the world—and a threat to teenagers everywhere.

ISIS is a Salifist extremist group that seeks to establish an Islamic country that encompasses most of the Middle East and

Opposite: ISIS recruits teenagers and young adults from around the world.

to govern that territory through their brutal interpretation of Sunni Islam. The group has been widely condemned by Muslims from around the world, and their extreme violence and ability to inspire terrorist activity in far flung areas has made them a concern to countries around the world. Their ideology is based heavily in the use of violence against non-Sunni Muslims or anyone who opposes them, and the group has often used young people to carry out that violence. They also believe in raising the next generation to believe fully in their ideology, which influences the way they recruit and use children and teenagers.

THE RISE OF ISIS

ISIS started as al-Qaeda's wing in Iraq in 2004, with the goal of fighting against US forces present in the country. The group came under the leadership of Abu Bakr al-Baghdadi, who currently leads ISIS, in 2010. When fighting broke out in Syria in 2011, interest shifted to the war-torn country and al-Baghdadi was given the task of establishing a Syrian wing for al-Qaeda, called al-Nusra Front.

Shortly thereafter, however, al-Baghdadi began clashing with al-Qaeda's leadership over tactics and goals, and he decided to break away from the core group to start his own extremist organization called Islamic State in Iraq and Syria, from which we get the name ISIS. The split was announced in 2013, and shortly thereafter ISIS began carrying out ethnic cleansing and violent attacks that won them territory in Syria and Iraq. Since then, the group has formed a de facto capital in Raqqa, Syria. And, despite being forced out of other territory by Iraqi military troops, they have continued

ISIS leader Abu Bakr al-Baghdadi is a highly secretive man, and has not been seen in public since 2014.

to carry out extreme violence and inspire terrorist attacks around the world.

ISIS is known for their extreme brutality, which plays a role in how they govern. The leadership uses large mass executions in public spaces to inspire fear in the people who live under their rule, and their propaganda is laced with threats against their enemies. In just a short amount of time, ISIS has become the leading extremist group in the world. And they work hard to maintain their support among young people.

When ISIS moved into eastern Syria, they quickly began targeting teenagers who had fought with or against Syrian President Bashar al-Assad. They used a combination of manipulation and force to make young people join their ranks through **indoctrination** and training. Ahmed was one of them. Although he fled the area as ISIS moved in, he soon found that living far from his family and friends as a young teen was too much emotionally. He told NBC News in 2015 that he was given assurances that he would not be hurt if he went home: "ISIS guaranteed if we returned, they would guarantee

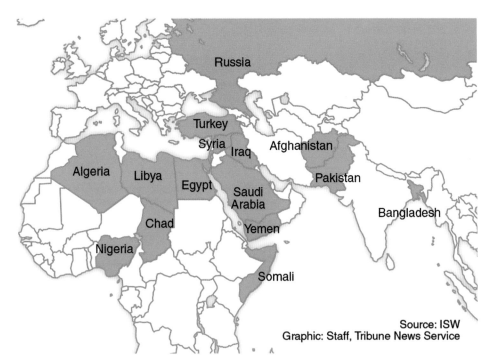

Source: ISW
Graphic: Staff, Tribune News Service

Although centered in Syria, ISIS operates in countries around the world. Countries with ISIS activity are shown here in red.

our safety," he said. "I needed to see my family. [ISIS] said if I go back, give up my weapon and that I wouldn't be harmed."

But ISIS had lied, and Ahmed was arrested shortly after he got back to his home town. In jail, he and the other teenagers and men he was being held with were tortured. "Many people died there," he said. After spending two months in prison, Ahmed was told he had to take part in classes and become a full fighter for ISIS, where they encouraged young boys to become suicide bombers: "They asked us, 'Who wants to be a martyr?' One of the boys who was with us, he was twelve years old. He blew himself up in an area called Haditha [in Iraq]."

Mohammed was thirteen years old when he was arrested and tortured by ISIS. He was told that he had to repent and go through re-education, an indoctrination program that Mohammed feared would end with him on the front lines. Instead, he tried to escape but was captured and punished. "[The judge] said to me, 'This is the judgment of God. You were going to the land of the infidels ... so you are like them. Your leg and arm must be cut off,'" Mohammed said.

RADICALIZATION AND SOCIAL MEDIA

ISIS doesn't simply recruit young people in their area. They also use social media to lure foreign fighters from around the world, including hundreds from the United States, the United Kingdom, and Europe. They are particularly interested in attracting teenagers, many of whom have been caught before they can board planes to destinations from which they can get to Syria.

Social media has proven one of the most effective ways ISIS can spread their propaganda, although the process of radicalization can be long and complicated. They identify potential recruits and engage them gradually, starting with listening to their problems before introducing the idea of joining ISIS as a way to take control of their lives. ISIS uses targeted recruiters to match the potential recruit. For teenage girls, the group uses female recruiters of a similar age, for example. ISIS promotes an image of themselves that can be appealing to teenagers. Life under the ISIS rule is presented as meaningful, heroic, and full of the promise of glory.

"The general picture provided by foreign fighters of their lives in Syria suggests camaraderie, good morale and purposeful activity, all mixed in with a sense of understated

Teenage girls have been targeted for ISIS recruitment. They are encouraged to travel to ISIS territory and marry ISIS fighters.

heroism, designed to attract their friends as well as to boost their own self-esteem," writes Richard Barrett in a report by the Soufan Group called "Foreign Fighters in Syria." As he points out, much of ISIS's propaganda is rooted in a sense of community, and they use it to prey on young people who feel isolated or alone. Posing as friends, the recruiter (who is paid a large amount of money if they succeed in drawing in new fighters) isolates them further by exploiting differences the recruit feels exist between them and their peers or family. For young Muslims, recruiters are able to play on concerns that the public sees them as terrorists already. These recruiters emphasize the teens' feelings of being an outsider. This is paired with an influx of attention from other ISIS supporters, creating the illusion of community. Author and professor Mia Bloom told *Marie Claire* how this creates an echo chamber and a sense of belonging:

> The moment you indicate any sort of interest in ISIS or ask any questions about it on a social platform, you get five hundred new followers on Twitter, you get five hundred friends on Facebook, you start getting emails and messages constantly—it's a kind of love bombing. All of a sudden, you feel really popular, important, and significant because of this flood of attention. And it all wraps up in the same ideology they message over and over: ISIS can give you something emotionally and psychologically that you will not have unless you come to the Islamic State.

These young people are then manipulated and encouraged to join the fight against the West, with ISIS posing it as a religious obligation in some cases. Recruits are given money and resources to help them get to Syria or encouraged to carry out attacks in their home countries if they are unable to travel.

OTHER REASONS FOR JOINING ISIS

The Khans were three siblings who tried to leave their home in a Chicago suburb to join ISIS in Syria. Mohammed Hamzah, the oldest, was nineteen. Mariyam, the only girl, was seventeen. Their younger brother, Tarek, was sixteen. They wrote letters to their family before leaving their home, but were stopped at O'Hare Airport before they could board their flight. Their case is a prime example of the way ISIS is able to play on a sense of moral obligation and teen angst to draw in teenage boys and girls of varied ages.

"They were naive, and they were sheltered, and they bought into a fantasy of a Muslim utopia," Marlo Cadeddu, Mariyam's attorney in the terrorism case brought against her by the US government, told *Rolling Stone*. "It's hard to be an observant Muslim teenager growing up in post-9/11 America, and ISIS plays on those insecurities in a very calculated way."

Some young people are brought to Syria by families who are joining ISIS, and soon after the children are made part of the group as well. According to John Horgan, a psychologist at Georgia State University who has studied the use of children by ISIS, in 2016 as many as 1,500 individuals under the age of eighteen were mobilized by ISIS between 2014 and 2016. He explained the process by which ISIS indoctrinates minors

Kadiza Sultana, Shamima Begum, and Amira Abase made headlines worldwide when they left their London homes to join ISIS in Syria in 2015.

as starting with toys or other gifts to make the children feel comfortable. But soon it progresses, as he told NPR in 2016:

> The next phase is schooling, and this is where kids are far more subject to intense indoctrination, which they don't really understand the ideology but they do parrot it. But it also brings the kids far closer to ISIS-specific personnel, so recruiters who are able to select kids out who might be showing aptitude for one activity or another. And this is where ISIS essentially creates prestige among these young kids at school. And they project the idea to them that greater things await should they be lucky enough to be accepted to go from the schools into a military training camp and stationed as part of the Islamic State's military activity.

For young people who change their minds, however, things can quickly turn deadly. As John Horgan said: "There are numerous accounts of children who failed at training or who miss their parents too much and decided that, you know, this really wasn't for them. In some cases, in many cases in fact, those children were severely beaten and, in some cases, even executed."

Just like the LRA forces young people to take part in violence to make them identify with the group, ISIS uses acts of violence as part of their brainwashing. Young people, sometimes as young as twelve, are made to take part in executions. One man, Ahmed al-Jabouri, fled Mosul after ISIS took control of the city. He told Al-Monitor that he had seen young people take an active role in the violence that followed ISIS's rise, "I once met one of these kids. He was Syrian and was as young as twelve years old. He was clad in black. His clothes were similar to the clothing worn by ISIS leader Abu Bakr al-Baghdadi when he made his first appearance back in July 2014. The young boy was at the forefront of a group that had executed a so-called apostate in one of Mosul's streets [in February]. The boy was the one to slaughter the victim with a knife."

RECRUITING TEENAGE GIRLS

ISIS also heavily recruits girls and women to join them, to serve as brides for fighters. In 2014, the group launched a campaign called "al-Zawra," which specifically targeted young women and teenage girls. ISIS also runs a marriage bureau for young women from the West, which advocates for marriage as young as nine and for girls to stop their education at fifteen years old.

Although they are promised a life of respect and care, these girls most often find something very different when they arrive. The lives of ISIS brides are hard and full of abuse, with a teenager girls married off to fighters quickly and repeatedly if their husbands die in battle. However, this reality does not seem to deter young women when they decide to join ISIS. In 2015, three fifteen-year-old girls left London to join ISIS in Syria. Khadiza Khanom, Amira Abase, and Shamima Begum had shown signs of becoming increasingly devout, but no one could guess that they had been in touch with ISIS recruiters and were making pacts to join the group. The girls were smart, independent, and actively engaged in their communities—but they were drawn to the propaganda image of ISIS as a place where women can meet and support devout men fighting for the future of Islam. Since arriving in Syria in 2015, the girls have been married to fighters and began recruiting other young women, much like Aqsa, a young woman who has become a key contact for teenage girls hoping to go to Syria.

Aqsa seemed like an average nineteen-year-old living in Scotland when she shocked her family by going to Syria. She has since become a recruiter for ISIS, focusing on getting teenage girls to go to the Middle East to marry ISIS fighters. She had a Tumblr that has since been shut down where she would chronicle her life and encourage other girls to join her in Syria.

While Aqsa often posted propaganda about her life under ISIS, she also gave glimpses of the overwhelming sadness of leaving her old life behind. On Mother's Day in 2014, she wrote:

I am writing this because I miss my mother, and I want this to be a reminder to all of you, to recognize the worth and value of your mother, because once you lose her, nothing will be the same again. While most of you can still see your mother's smile, I cannot anymore. While most of you can still put your head on your mom's shoulder, I cannot anymore. While most of you can still call out to your mother when you feel pain in your body, I cannot anymore. While most of you can still go and have that heart to heart talk with your mother, I cannot anymore.

STOPPING RECRUITMENT

Finding ways to stop the recruitment of teenagers by ISIS has been challenging for governments. Efforts to spread awareness of what reality under ISIS is like have been undertaken by local groups and national organizations alike. Outreach targeting those who are more vulnerable to recruitment can help get young people out of the cycle before it's too late. Even so, with each young person caught at the airport trying to get to Syria, it is more and more clear that it will take much larger efforts to fully stop ISIS recruitment strategies. "It's a war of ideas—we ought to be able to win," Assistant Attorney General John Carlin said in 2015. "How do we explain that an ideology that's based on enslaving other people, killing women and children … is one you shouldn't join?"

Lisa Monaco, a former presidential assistant for homeland security and counterterrorism, says more needs to be done at an earlier stage and within communities to get at the root reasons why teens join ISIS, telling the *Washington Post*, "We need to do more to help communities understand the warning signs and then work together to intervene before an incident can occur."

Countries also struggle with how best to prosecute young people who try to join ISIS or who escape. Although leaving them unpunished undermines the gravity of the choice they made, they are also victims of manipulation and deception. This is particularly true for young people who never make it to Syria or carry out attacks on behalf of ISIS, such as the Khan children. Mohammed Hamzah's attorney, Tom Durkin, argues that prosecuting young people like the Khans does little to work against recruitment and rather plays into the negative side of the "War on Terror." "The fact is, these kids are not 'terrorists' by any criminal-justice definition," Durkin told *Rolling Stone*. "The problem is, it's now part of the 'war on terror,' and as soon as you declare war on something, that means you have to defeat it."

THE INTERNATIONAL IMPACT OF ISIS RECRUITMENT

The impact of ISIS's recruitment of teenagers can be felt around the world. With hundreds of teens leaving the EU, Australia, the UK, and the US, finding ways to bring their recruitment to an end is crucial but difficult. It is changing the way we think about terrorist recruitment and its appeal for young people. If a teenager who seems to be living a normal life can be seduced by an ideology as violent as that of ISIS, what needs are not being met by their life at home that ISIS purports to be able to meet?

Fears about teenage recruits are also impacting the refugee crisis. It is believed that hundreds—if not thousands—of teenagers with EU passports are fighting in Syria and could return to carry out attacks. While concern about potential terrorists traveling as refugees has been proved to be unfounded, concerns that teenagers could be asked to return to their home countries for the purpose of carrying out attacks has been a driving force in rising anti-immigration sentiments across Europe. Yet ultimately these fears hide the real concern, which is ensuring that young people do not feel the need to join ISIS or are given ways to leave the group safely when they change their mind. Meeting their complex mental and physical health

These ISIS and Al-Nusra recruiters were arrested in Russia in 2017.

needs must be a priority if these young people and others who hope to leave the group are going to be given another chance at life.

It is important to take into consideration why and how ISIS is able to recruit young people. By preying on their sense of alienation, isolation, or desire to do good in the world, ISIS is able to create a sense of connection to the group's mission. To do so, the group also has to promote a very specific image of what life under their rule is like. But given the widespread coverage of ISIS's violence, it is hard to say if campaigns that debunk their myths are effective. Instead, it is important to create opportunities for young people to connect with their communities, feel supported, and be heard so that they feel they have a place in society.

CHAPTER FIVE

Looking Ahead

Teenagers have been recruited by terrorist organizations for as long as terrorist organizations have existed, and there is little reason to think these groups will stop targeting young people to join them. But that doesn't mean that there is nothing that can be done to combat recruitment of teenagers. In fact, a lot is being done by governments and international organizations around the world.

WHAT'S AT STAKE

Teenagers are a primary source of manpower for terrorist organizations. They are able to take on heavy manual labor and attacks, while often being healthy enough to need little in medical care. Cutting off recruitment would be a significant blow to operations for groups like the LRA and ISIS.

Opposite: Young terrorist recruits face an uphill battle when it comes to rejoining communities and moving forward. Pictured is a member of a Sri Lankan terrorist group called the Tamil Tigers.

Young people who join terrorist organizations often live through harrowing experiences that leave lasting mental scars. According to a report by the United States Institute for Peace, this can involve:

> Repeated and thus cumulative effects of traumatic stress, exposure to combat, shelling and other life-threatening events, acts of abuse, such as torture or rape, violent death of a parent or friend, witnessing family members being tortured or injured, separation from family, being abducted or held in detention, insufficient adult care, lack of safe drinking water and food, inadequate shelter, explosive devices and dangerous building ruins in the proximity, marching or being transported in crowded vehicles over long distances, and spending months in transit camps.

Issues like PTSD, depression, severe anxiety, and other mental health problems can make engaging with day-to-day life difficult for these young people, and they need professional help to work through their trauma. Grief or guilt for what they have taken part in can also be an issue in self-esteem and self-worth, giving them a negative view of themselves and their lives.

Many young people are also recovering from exposure to drugs or other substances that were used by groups to alter or control their behavior. The LRA and ISIS routinely drug combatants to make them less afraid, getting them addicted to drugs like opium or heroin. K. K. G. was just thirteen when he joined the Mai-Mai in the Democratic Republic of Congo.

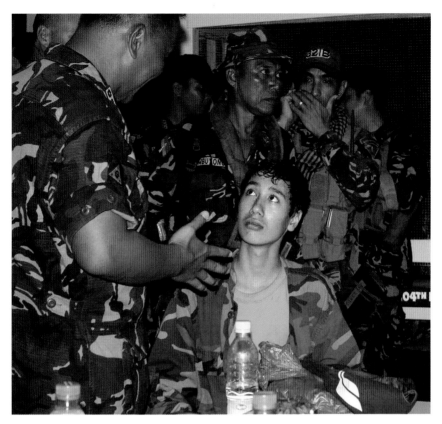

Kevin Lunsman is an American teen who was kidnapped by terrorists while on vacation in the Philippines. His story shows that teens can be victims of terrorist groups in numerous ways.

At sixteen years old, he was living with the high mental cost of having taken part in atrocities, which he was numbed to by the use of drugs:

When I was out in the forest, I was feeling nothing, I was drugged all the time. But after I had come out and now since I stay in this transit center, I get these terrible nightmares. They are always about the children we killed … and I hear the voice of my commander telling me to do things. I wake up and get so frightened. My heart is beating strong these days and something in my head is so wrong. On one hand, I have a new life and I have left the forest behind and also all the hardship of those days, on the other, I think of the times and especially the drugs we had. Sometimes at night I walk out of the building, especially when I get the dreams and stare at the sky. I would just wish that my head gets normal again.

With the exception of ISIS, which recruits from around the world, the countries where teenagers are most at risk for terrorist recruitment also often struggle with poverty and lack of opportunity. Although we often think of the impact serving with terrorist groups can have on people at a young age, the impact can be wide ranging. With thousands of young people taking part in combat around the world, it is important to note that their countries of origin or host countries can also suffer as a result, as Christopher Blattman and Jeannie Annan argue in a report written for the University of Sussex Institute of Development studies:

This concern is a critical one for post-conflict economic development, as adverse impacts on education can take years to recover and damage to health may not recover at all. With so many millions of young ex-combatants, such damage to human capital could therefore hinder their nations' productivity and growth for decades. Moreover, any impact of military service on inequality, aggression and political alienation could threaten a nation's long term stability and growth.

Therefore, several things need to happen to help former recruits, like providing mental health care and substance abuse treatment. Creating economic growth is also key. Opportunities are crucial to breaking the cycle of violence and disillusionment that allows terrorist groups to thrive and prey on young people in the first place.

Ending Recruitment for Good

In many places around the world, terrorist recruitment is a complex blend of need and manipulation. Groups like Hezbollah, the Muslim Brotherhood, or the Tamil Tigers are able to meet needs the government cannot, giving them a high level of public support despite their terrorist activities. This can lead young people to believe that joining one of these or other organizations is about supporting their community and helping their family rather than becoming a terrorist. In the Philippines, one teen who joined MILF told UNICEF that he felt lucky to have joined the group because he might have been forced to rely on gang activity to make ends meet otherwise. One young man, who was twelve when he joined rebels in Myanmar, looked back on his time with the group at age twenty-four and still saw it as a positive experience:

> Thinking back, it was a good experience for me. If I had stayed in the town, without enough food I might have had to do something bad, such as stealing or something like that. Now I think more about studying, continuing

my education. Now my aim is not to be a soldier but to do other things. I would like to go to Bible school.

Although these kinds of positive experiences are rare, the needs that are highlighted by them are not. Economic and community development are crucial to making terrorist groups less appealing. Providing young people with opportunity, security, and care will make them less likely to become disillusioned with their societies and less likely to be receptive to the messages used by terrorist organizations to recruit them.

In the United States, privacy often chafes against the need to keep an eye on anyone who could become a terrorist recruit. In most cases the government gets involved at the later stages of recruitment, such as when a teenager puts into action a

Social media companies have worked to limit the reach of groups like ISIS, but social media is still an effective recruitment tool.

plan to leave the country and join ISIS. Although this stops them from joining the group in Syria or elsewhere, it does not address the underlying reasons why they were radicalized or work towards **deradicalization**, an important step if the young person is going to disavow the extremist teachings they had been willing to subscribe to.

Abdullahi Yusuf was eighteen years old and living in Minneapolis when he was caught at the airport trying to board a plane to Turkey. The FBI stopped him and sent him home. Having watched him for around a month, agents were aware of his intentions to join ISIS. Before returning to his home, Yusuf sent a tweet that read "The weather is hot today," a message to other recruits and his handlers with ISIS to let them know he had been caught. Several months later, he was arrested on terrorism-related charges.

This case highlights the inherent flaws in this method of intervention. Yusuf had already been radicalized, and simply stopping him at the airport did not change that. Instead, if intervention can happen earlier, young people can be convinced not to join ISIS and brought back into the fold of their communities much more quickly.

IMPROVING DERADICALIZATION PRACTICES

The process of deradicalization is complex but important. Daniel Koehler is a researcher who began his career working with former neo-Nazis, and has since become an expert in deradicalization programs targeting former Islamic extremists. What he has found is that although countries from Saudi

Arabia to Denmark have deradicalization programs, there is little uniformity among them. "The deradicalization field globally is more or less completely free of any working standards, which is insane," Koehler told *Wired* in 2017. "Many of these counselors, they do things because they feel right, but they can't explain to you why. They have no training, no handbooks, no anything."

Koehler has been working to change that, and to introduce a standard, science-based process to the field of deradicalization. Koehler believes that redirecting the attention of potential recruits can make a difference, and he advocates for the gradual introduction of small-scale concerns that show the flaws of joining a terrorist group. This can be as small as pointing out that if they go to Syria, they will be taking food that could help an orphan. Koehler's plans are controversial, with many people concerned that his multi-year process isn't realistic. However, Koehler has been doing important work around the globe to change the way we approach radicalization. Through interviews, he is also working to better understand why teens are recruited. "These teenagers, they are intrigued by the promise that they will immediately start to change society and live out their ideals," he told *Wired*. "For them, these movements are about freedom and justice and honoring their values." It's a sentiment that other people who work with former recruits echo. "The more we learn about ISIS, the more we know how to prevent terrorism," Maya Yamout, a Lebanese social worker who works with former ISIS recruits, told the *Huffington Post*. "The solution to halt their recruitment begins first with awareness, and then prevention."

"Terrorists I interviewed confirmed that there is an ISIS recruiting agent in every corner in the world today. They prey on the vulnerable ones," Yamout continued. "Those who are poor, they persuade them with money. Those with psychological troubles, they provide them with drugs."

Understanding how ISIS recruits young people—and how they treat them after the fact—is key to making sure authorities are able to undermine their efforts. Terrorist organizations around the world rely on lies and manipulation to attract and keep young recruits, preying on their fear and worry to make them think they are only safe when with the group and following orders. This amounts to emotional abuse and can make it difficult for young people to summon the courage to escape.

Work to combat this manipulation is undertaken by groups like Invisible Children, a group that works against the LRA. Invisible Children works with formerly abducted fighters to record messages that are broadcast throughout areas where the LRA is active. These messages encourage young people to escape and return home, going against the LRA's efforts to make their captives believe they will be killed or harmed if they do so.

While learning from young people who have been directly in contact with such groups is an important part of this work, it is just as important to make sure that the safety of the individual is the top priority, not intelligence gathering. Dr. Lorenzo Vidino of the Program on Extremism at George Washington University wrote in the *Washington Post*, "Young people undergoing a process of radicalization are seen as vulnerable individuals harming themselves and ultimately in need of help. Radicalization is presented as a problem like gang recruitment or drugs. Just as they would do if they detected young people falling prey to such social ills, community leaders have a responsibility to report cases of radicalization."

REINTEGRATING VICTIMS INTO SOCIETY

As we've seen, young people who have been abducted or voluntarily joined terrorist organizations face an uphill battle when it comes to reintegrating into their former communities. In the case of teenagers who were abducted by the LRA, some of them have no families to return to or fear punishment or isolation if they do so.

Many teens who join terrorist organizations miss out on crucial years of education or access to training opportunities,

A young South Sudanese soldier at a 2015 ceremony celebrating the reintegration of child soldiers into society

making it difficult to find employment and build a stable life. Overcoming that obstacle is crucial. Re-recruitment is more common among those who are not able to become financially and socially independent. It is also important to recognize that their behavior can be shaped by their mental state, and it could lead to stigmatization, USIP says.

USIP's research shows that trauma and depression can manifest as outward behaviors that may look like aggression or just bad behavior. If young people are not given ways to express themselves and deal with the conflicting emotions they are experiencing, this kind of behavior can make taking part in education, the workforce, or just normal relationships extremely difficult. Recognizing these behaviors and finding ways to help young people cope with them can go a long way in making their reintegration easier, and by association help them carry on with their lives.

One teen who joined a terrorist group in Papua New Guinea at the age of nine experienced this kind of aggression and violence after his time as a fighter, telling UNICEF:

Now when I'm very cross with someone, I easily black out and when I black out I use whatever is in my hands to fight—to cause injury—without realizing what's happening. I can't listen to anyone trying to control me or tell me what to do. Afterward, it will take time to realize what I've done. There have been two instances: I shot my sister in a quarrel in the right arm. She was fighting with my father. My father was complaining that my sister did not listen to my father's advice. I just got up and shot her. She could have died.

Someone pushed the gun as I fired it. Another time, a man stole some trousers and was caught. I took his hand and said, "You use these fingers to steal." And I chopped off his finger.

To help them adjust to civilian life, it is important to provide outlets for teen terrorist recruits to process what they have experienced. In many cases, including that of V. O., who spoke to the USIP about his time with the LRA, being able to speak with others who have gone through similar circumstances can help them understand their emotions and face the future with hope.

I often think of all these children out there who still suffer and try to survive. So many people out there went through the same thing as I did. When I go through town here, there are so many children I recognize from the bush and they recognize me. Those who know me from the bush when we meet say, "We came back, and now you are also back, who would have thought?" If they can manage, I can also survive. When you ask me about five years from now where I would like to be in life, then I say, if all goes very well I will survive and be alive.

PUTTING IT ALL TOGETHER

Teenagers who join terrorist organizations do so for a variety of reasons. Some of them are abducted or forced to take up arms and then manipulated through fear to stay loyal to the group. Others join voluntarily because they fear for themselves or their families and they see in terrorist organizations a way toward a better future. No matter why they join, however, most teenagers who do so soon find that the reality of living on the run from authorities and under fire from combatants is not heroic or glorious. It is jarring, violent, and terrifying. Forced into situations that most adults would be afraid of, these young people survive despite the odds and sometimes manage to escape.

When they do, they are faced with the struggle to adjust to civilian life after living through extraordinary experiences. Concerns about their mental health, physical well being, long-term education, and ability to reintegrate into society are numerous, and it is crucial that they get into programs designed to help them deradicalize and adjust quickly.

But at the end of the day, these young people are just like any other. They want a bright future where they feel safe and loved, with every opportunity to achieve

Young combatants, like this Ethiopian boy, require quick and effective treatment to overcome their violent past and secure a promising future.

WHO IS RESPONSIBLE?

Holding people accountable is an important part of the healing process following civil war, genocide, and other mass-casualty events that divide countries. This is no less true of teen terrorist recruits. The leaders who allowed teens and young people to be recruited into fighting forces must be held accountable. Their accountability is crucial to helping communities move forward. But the question of guilt is a complex one when talking about teenage terrorist recruits. On one hand, some teens made a choice to join an organization that engages in terrorist activity. Yet in many cases, they are abducted or otherwise coerced and often do not fully understand what they are signing up for. This is particularly true of teenagers under the age of fifteen, an age group that studies have found is especially susceptible to recruitment.

Whether or not young people can be held truly accountable for the actions they carry out when with a terrorist organization is difficult to say. While they must take some level of responsibility for the act itself, in situations when they are forced or feel as if they are in danger if they do not commit an act of violence, the lines between victim and criminal are blurred. It is also difficult to say whether traditional punishments, including prison, are the best way to help these young people overcome the indoctrination they experienced and the events they witnessed.

their goals. As one young girl who joined a terrorist group in the Philippines told UNICEF, she just wants a normal and happy life: "I now want to finish school, to have a job. I want to be a teacher. Those are things that I hope for. I realize that I can change my life. I want to lead a peaceful life."

apartheid Laws and systems put in place to ensure discrimination and segregation of a certain group in society.

autonomous An area that is largely independent with some control over its own laws and borders but has ties to a larger government.

child soldier A military or other armed recruit under the age of consent, which is eighteen for most countries and in some cases as young as sixteen.

common identity A set of experiences, cultural beliefs, or values that unites a group or country, creating a sense of loyalty and belonging.

conscription Mandatory enlistment in armed forces, usually for citizens.

Convention on the Rights of the Child International treaty outlining the rights of children, including the political and social obligations states have to children within their borders.

crimes against humanity Actions that lead to widespread suffering or death, such as genocide.

deradicalization A process by which radicalization is undone.

ethnic cleansing A deliberate program of violence or intimidation aimed at forcing an "unwanted" ethnic or religious group to leave an area.

existential threat Something that poses danger to an individual's existence.

freedom fighter An individual who uses irregular warfare techniques to achieve political goals.

Geneva Conventions International treaties passed in 1949 that outline laws regarding conflict, treatment of civilians, and other wartime matters.

indoctrination Teaching an individual beliefs in a way that does not encourage them to think critically or question them.

international statutes International laws considered binding between states and inside nations.

Irish Republican Army (IRA) An armed movement that agitated for independence in Ireland and Northern Ireland in the twentieth century.

ISIS Islamic State; a terrorist organization based in Syria and Iraq led by Abu Bakr al-Baghdadi.

Lord's Resistance Army (LRA) A terrorist organization led by Joseph Kony that was established in northern Uganda.

militias Loosely or highly organized armed groups that are not formally part of a country's military.

non-state actors Groups or individuals that are not part of the formal power structure of a country but have significant influence and power.

Optional Protocol to the Convention on the Rights of the Child Additions to the Convention on the Rights of the Child, including raising the age limit for military recruitment to the age of eighteen. These are non-binding resolutions.

post-traumatic stress disorder (PTSD) A disorder brought on by traumatic experiences, which can manifest as depression, aggression, flashbacks, anxiety, or other symptoms.

radicalization The process by which an individual is made to identify with and accept radical, extremist views.

Salifist A school of Islamic thought that advocates for a return to a way of life considered more true to that of "devout" early followers of Islam.

sovereign state An independent state with control of its own laws and borders.

Tamil Tigers Sri Lankan terrorist organization seeking an independent Tamil state in the north east.

terrorism The use of violence and fear to achieve political goals.

terrorist organization A domestic, regional, or international group that engages in activity that could be considered terrorism, with political motivations.

tribal Relating to a group or community identity rather than a national identity.

war crimes Actions undertaken during a conflict that violent international law, such as torture of prisoners of war.

FURTHER INFORMATION

Books

Beah, Ishmael. *A Long Way Gone: Memoirs of a Boy Soldier.* New York: Sarah Crichton Books, 2008.

Erelle, Anna. *In the Skin of a Jihadist: A Young Journalist Enters the ISIS Recruitment Network.* New York: HarperCollins, 2015.

Kamal, Soniah. *An Isolated Incident.* New Delhi, India: Prakash Book Depot, 2014.

Lalami, Laila. *Secret Son.* New York: Algonquin Books, 2010.

Websites

Invisible Children

http://www.invisiblechildren.com

This organization works to save young people abducted by the LRA. On their website, find more information about the threat of the LRA and also find ways to help.

UNICEF

http://www.unicef.org

Read the latest information about teen terrorist recruits, and find out how UNICEF helps young people around the world.

Videos

"ISIS 'Aggressively' Recruiting from Minnesota"

https://www.youtube.com/watch?v=9Aerd-4M7e8

CNN takes a closer look at how ISIS and al-Shabaab recruit teens from the United States.

"ISIS Uses Social Media to Increase Western Recruitment"

https://www.youtube.com/watch?v=wObRO6jwrA4&spfre load=10

Learn more about the role social media sites play in the recruitment of teen terrorists in this report from CBS Morning News.

Bennhold, Katrin. "Jihad and Girl Power: How ISIS Lured 3 London Girls." *New York Times*, August 17, 2015. https://www.nytimes.com/2015/08/18/world/europe/ jihad-and-girl-power-how-isis-lured-3-london-teenagers. html?_r=0.

Blattman, Christoper, and Jeannie Annan. "The Consequences of Child Soldiering." The Institute of Development Studies, August 2007. http://www.hicn.org/ wordpress/wp-content/uploads/2012/06/wp22.pdf.

Brett, Rachel. "Girl Soldiers: Challenging Assumptions." Quaker United Nations Office, November 5, 2002. http:// www.quno.org/sites/default/files/resources/Girl%20 Soldiers_Challenging%20the%20assumptions.pdf.

Conde, Carlos H. "Dispatches: Fighting Over Child Soldiers in the Philippines." Human Rights Watch, February 16, 2016. https://www.hrw.org/news/2016/02/16/dispatches-fighting-over-child-soldiers-philippines.

De Castro, Elizabeth Protacio. "Children in Armed Conflict Situations: Focus on Child Soldiers in the Philippines." *Philippine Journal of Third World Studies*, 2001. http://journals.upd.edu.ph/index.php/kasarinlan/article/view/1649.

Dorian, Geiger. "This is How ISIS Uses Social Media to Recruit American Teens." *Teen Vogue*, November 20, 2015. http://www.teenvogue.com/story/isis-recruits-american-teens.

Fantz, Ashley, and Atika Shubert. "From Scottish Teen to ISIS Bride and Recruiter: the Aqsa Mahmood Story." CNN, February 24, 2015. http://www.cnn.com/2015/02/23/world/scottish-teen-isis-recruiter/.

Gonchar, Michael, and Katherine Schulten. "Teenagers and Extremism: Investigating the ISIS Recruitment Pipeline." *New York Times*, March 11, 2015. https://learning.blogs.nytimes.com/2015/03/11/teenagers-and-extremism-investigating-the-isis-recruitment-pipeline/?_r=0.

Hancock, Stephanie. "Witness: Abducted from School and Forced to Fight in South Sudan's War." Human Rights Watch, December 15, 2015. https://www.hrw.org/ news/2015/12/15/witness-abducted-school-and-forced-fight-south-sudans-war.

Haq, Husna. "ISIS Excels at Recruiting American Teens: Here Are Four Reasons Why." *Christian Science Monitor*, October 22, 2014. http://www.csmonitor.com/USA/USA-Update/2014/1022/ISIS-excels-at-recruiting-American-teens-Here-are-four-reasons-why-video.

Human Rights Watch. "We Can Die Too: Recruitment and Use of Child Soldiers in South Sudan." December 14, 2015. https://www.hrw.org/report/2015/12/14/we-can-die-too/recruitment-and-use-child-soldiers-south-sudan.

Kaplan, Eben. "Child Soldiers Around the World." Council on Foreign Relations, December 2, 2005. http://www.cfr. org/human-rights/child-soldiers-around-world/p9331.

Keairns, Yvonne E. "The Voices of Girl Child Soldiers. Quaker United Nations Office, January 2003. http://www. quno.org/sites/default/files/resources/The%20voices%20 of%20girl%20child%20soldiers_PHILIPPINES.pdf.

Koerner, Brendan L. "Can you Turn a Terrorist Back into a Citizen?" *Wired*, January 2017. https://www.wired.com/2017/01/can-you-turn-terrorist-back-into-citizen/.

Mark, Monica. "Joseph Kony Child Soldier Returns to Terrorised Boyhood Village." *The Guardian*, July 22, 2013. https://www.theguardian.com/world/2013/jul/23/joseph-kony-child-soldier-return-uganda-lra.

McDonald, Henry. "Terrorists Recruit Teenage Soldiers." *The Guardian*, October 23, 1999. https://www.theguardian.com/uk/1999/oct/24/northernireland.theobserver.

NPR. "ISIS Increasingly Recruiting Children to Carry Out Terrorist Acts." August 28, 2016. http://www.npr.org/2016/08/28/491699567/isis-child-soldiers.

Reitman, Janet. "The Children of ISIS." *Rolling Stone*, March 25, 2015. http://www.rollingstone.com/culture/features/teenage-jihad-inside-the-world-of-american-kids-seduced-by-isis-20150325.

Samuel, Thomas Koruth. "The Lure of Youth into Terrorism." Southeast Asia Regional Centre for Counterterrorism. Retrieved June 1, 2017. http://www.searcct.gov.my/publications/our-publications?id=55.

Schauer, Elisabeth, and Thomas Elbert. "The Psychological Impact of Child Soldiering." USIP. Retrieved April 1, 2017. https://www.usip.org/sites/default/files/missing-peace/The%20psychological%20impact%20of%20child%20soldiering%20-%20Schauer.pdf.

SOS Children's Villages. "A Former Child Soldier in Syria Tells His Story." March 2016. http://www.sos-usa.org/blog/march-2016/a-former-child-soldier-in-syria-tells-his-story.

Storey, Kate. "The American Women of ISIS." *Marie Claire*, April 22, 2016. http://www.marieclaire.com/politics/a20011/western-women-who-join-isis/.

Storr, Will. "Kony's Child Soldier." *The Telegraph*, February 12, 2014. http://www.telegraph.co.uk/news/worldnews/africaandindianocean/uganda/10621792/Konys-child-soldiers-When-you-kill-for-the-first-time-you-change.html.

UNICEF. "Adult Wars, Child Soldiers." October 2002. https://www.unicef.org/eapro/AdultWarsChildSoldiers.pdf.

United Nations Office of the Special Representative of the Secretary-General for Children and Armed

Conflict. "Philippines." April 20, 2016. https://
childrenandarmedconflict.un.org/countries-caac/
philippines/.

Voices of Youth. "Liberating Child Soldiers in the
Philippines." 2011. http://www.voicesofyouth.org/posts/
liberating-child-soldiers-in-the-philippines--2.

WBUR. "Former Kony Child Soldier Tells Her Story."
April 19, 2012. http://hereandnow.legacy.wbur.
org/2012/04/19/kony-child-soldier.

INDEX

Page numbers in **boldface** are illustrations. Entries in **boldface** are glossary terms.

Duterte, Rodrigo, 51

education, 7, 20, 39–40,
     42–43, 57, 69, 74, 84,
     86, 90–91, 93
empowerment, 55–57
ethnic cleansing, 66
execution, 67, 74
existential threat, 15

fear, 7, 12, 24–25, 28, 30,
     35–38, 40, 42, 54–55,
     57–58, 67, 69, 78,
     89–90, 92–93
food, 7, 16, 22, 29–30,
     32–33, 57, 60, 82,
     85, 88
freedom fighter, 14, 51

Geneva Conventions,
     9–10
girls, 6–7, 15–16, 22, 30,
     32–36, 41, 52, 54–57,
     56, 61–62, 70, **70**, 72,
     74–75, 95

guilt, 7, 31, 34, 82, 94

hunger, 33

ideology, 47, 66, 71, 73,
     76, 78
indoctrination, 68–69,
     72–73, 94
international statutes, 9
Invisible Children, 39, 89
Iran-Iraq War, 20
**Irish Republican Army
     (IRA)**, 15–16, 18
ISIS, 7, **9**, 16, 18, 23–24,
     29, 51, **64**, 65–79, **70**,
     81–82, 84, 87–89

Koehler, Daniel, 87–88
Kony, Joseph, 27–29, **28**

**Lord's Resistance Army
     (LRA)**, 7, 16, 27–43,
     27, **30**, 48, 55, 74,
     81–82, 89–90, 92

Bridey Heing is a writer and book critic based in Washington, DC. She holds degrees in political science and international affairs from DePaul University and Washington University in Saint Louis. Her areas of focus are comparative politics and Iranian politics. Her master's thesis explores the evolution of populist politics and democracy in Iran since 1900. She has written about Iranian affairs, women's rights, and art and politics for publications like the *Economist*, *Hyperallergic*, and the *Establishment*. She also writes about literature and film. She enjoys traveling, reading, and exploring Washington's many museums.